THE MEGA ATTRACTOR ORACLE

Sheila Galle Espejo

This oracle is a creative work designed for guidance purposes. It is not intended to replace professional advice or services.

Illustrations by AI

How to use this oracle

I've created this oracle with the aim of providing a tool you can use on a daily basis as a reminder of how incredibly magnetic you are. It offers a mix of educational, inspiring, and guiding messages.

I strongly believe we are constantly guided, often without being aware of it. My hope is that this book will serve as a physical reminder of that connection, and as a learning tool to become your most magnetic self.

I suggest using it every morning, right after waking up. Keep it somewhere visible so that you don't forget about it. Run your fingers over the pages and open it when it feels right. That will be the message for the day.

Feel free to share your experience with me on Instagram (@sheilagalleespejo). I'd love to hear your thoughts!

AUTHENTICITY IS THE MOST ATTRACTING ENERGY THERE IS.

WHAT CAN I DO TODAY TO BE MY MOST AUTHENTIC SELF?

WHAT'S MY FREQUENCY NOW, AND WHAT'S THE FREQUENCY OF THE PERSON I WANT TO BECOME?

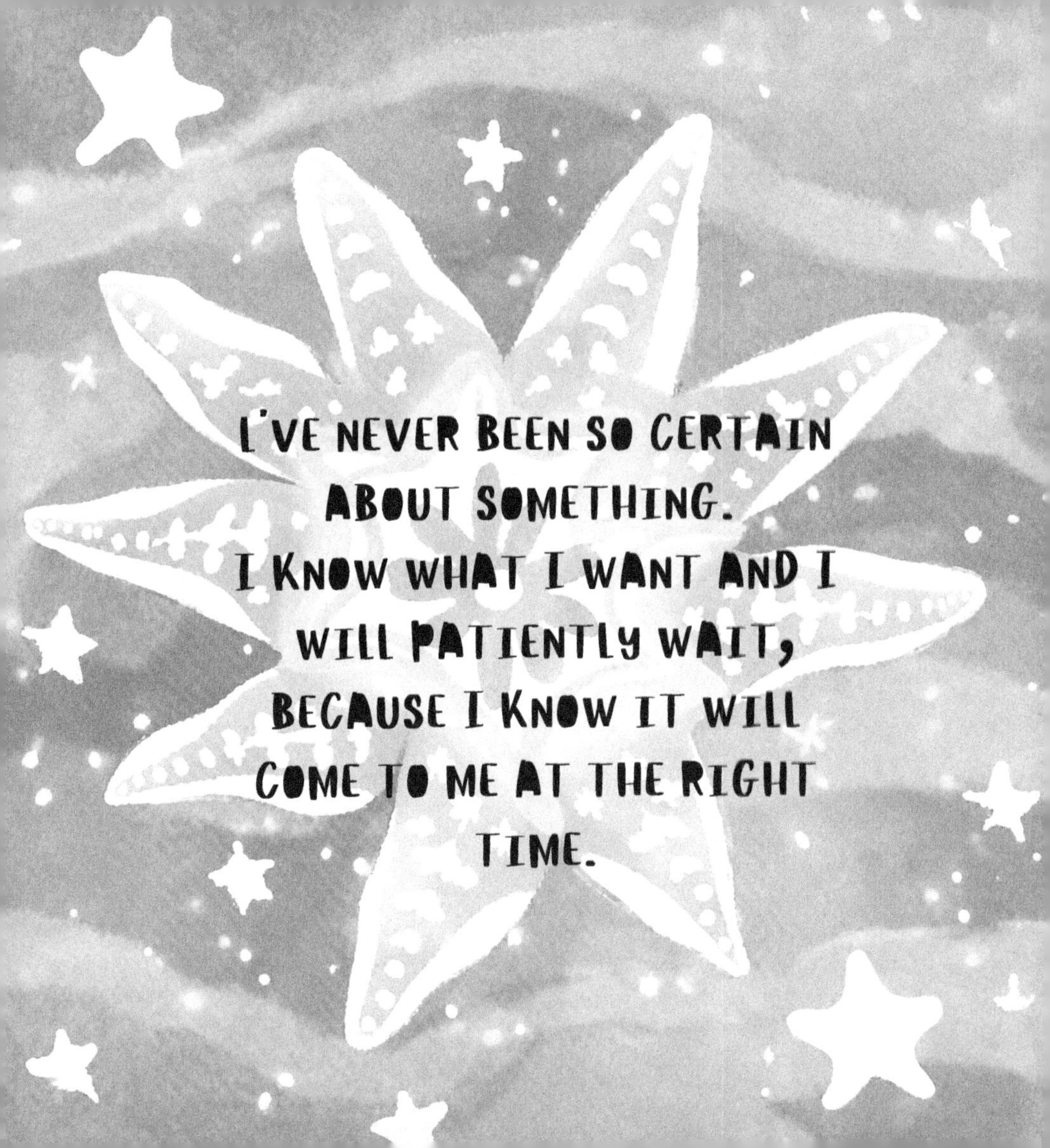

I'VE NEVER BEEN SO CERTAIN ABOUT SOMETHING. I KNOW WHAT I WANT AND I WILL PATIENTLY WAIT, BECAUSE I KNOW IT WILL COME TO ME AT THE RIGHT TIME.

MY STRESS AND DISAPPOINTMENT
COMES FROM BEING IN A HURRY.
I TRUST THAT EVERYTHING COMES AT
THE RIGHT TIME. I FIND PEACE IN WHO
I AM
AND RELEASE TENSION FROM WHO I
THINK I SHOULD BE.
WHAT'S MEANT FOR ME WILL COME TO
ME AT THE RIGHT TIME. IT ALWAYS
DOES.

I MANIFEST WHEN I AM
PRESENT AND AT PEACE

I TRUST THE PROCESS.
I AM MEANT TO GET THERE.
ALL I NEED TO DO IS BELIEVE.
I KNOW WHERE I AM HEADED.
I LET 'THE HOW' BE PART OF MY GUIDANCE.

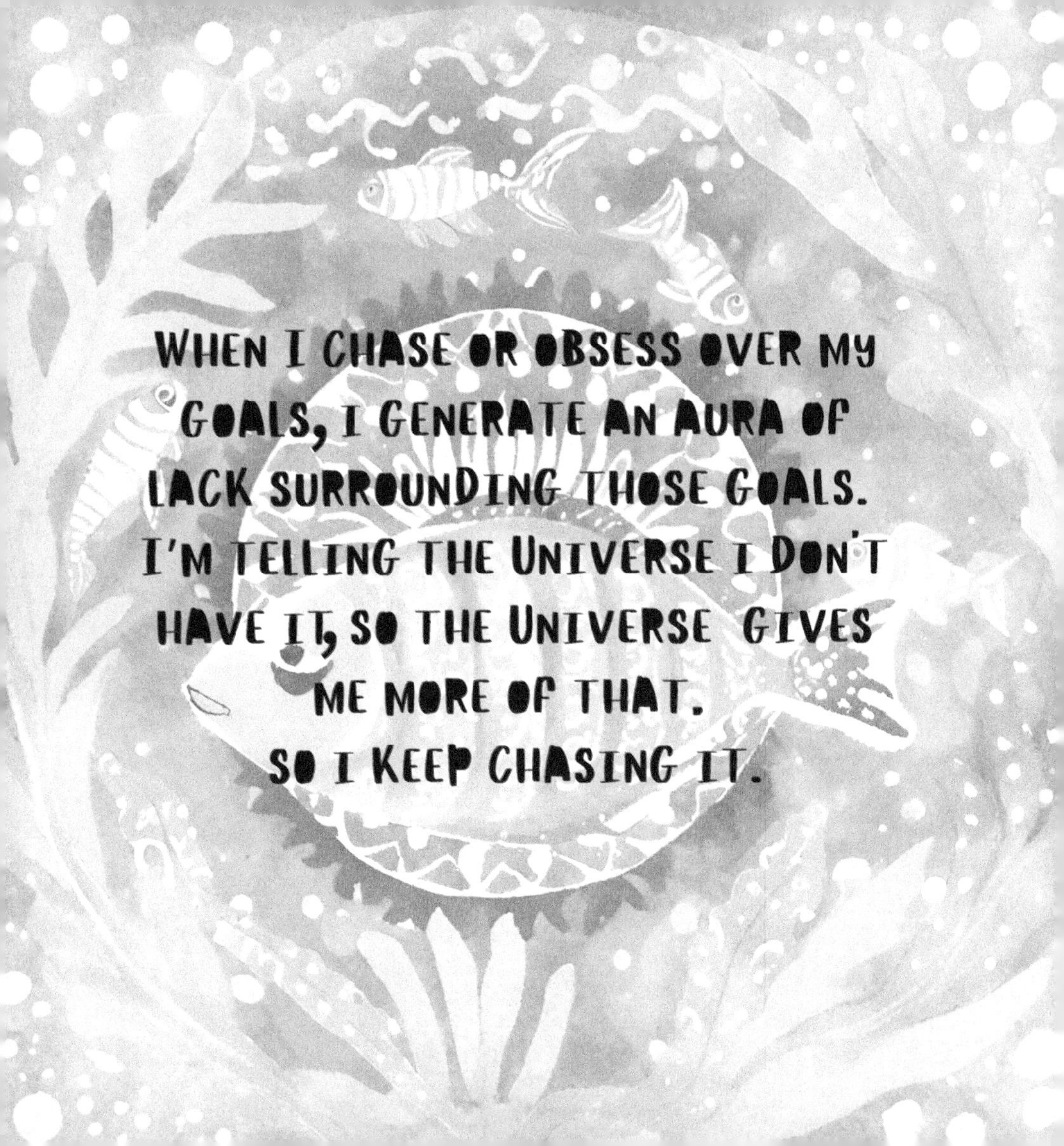

WHEN I CHASE OR OBSESS OVER MY GOALS, I GENERATE AN AURA OF LACK SURROUNDING THOSE GOALS. I'M TELLING THE UNIVERSE I DON'T HAVE IT, SO THE UNIVERSE GIVES ME MORE OF THAT. SO I KEEP CHASING IT.

IF I CAN IMAGINE IT,
IT CAN EXIST.

IF I CAN FEEL IT,
IT WILL EXIST.

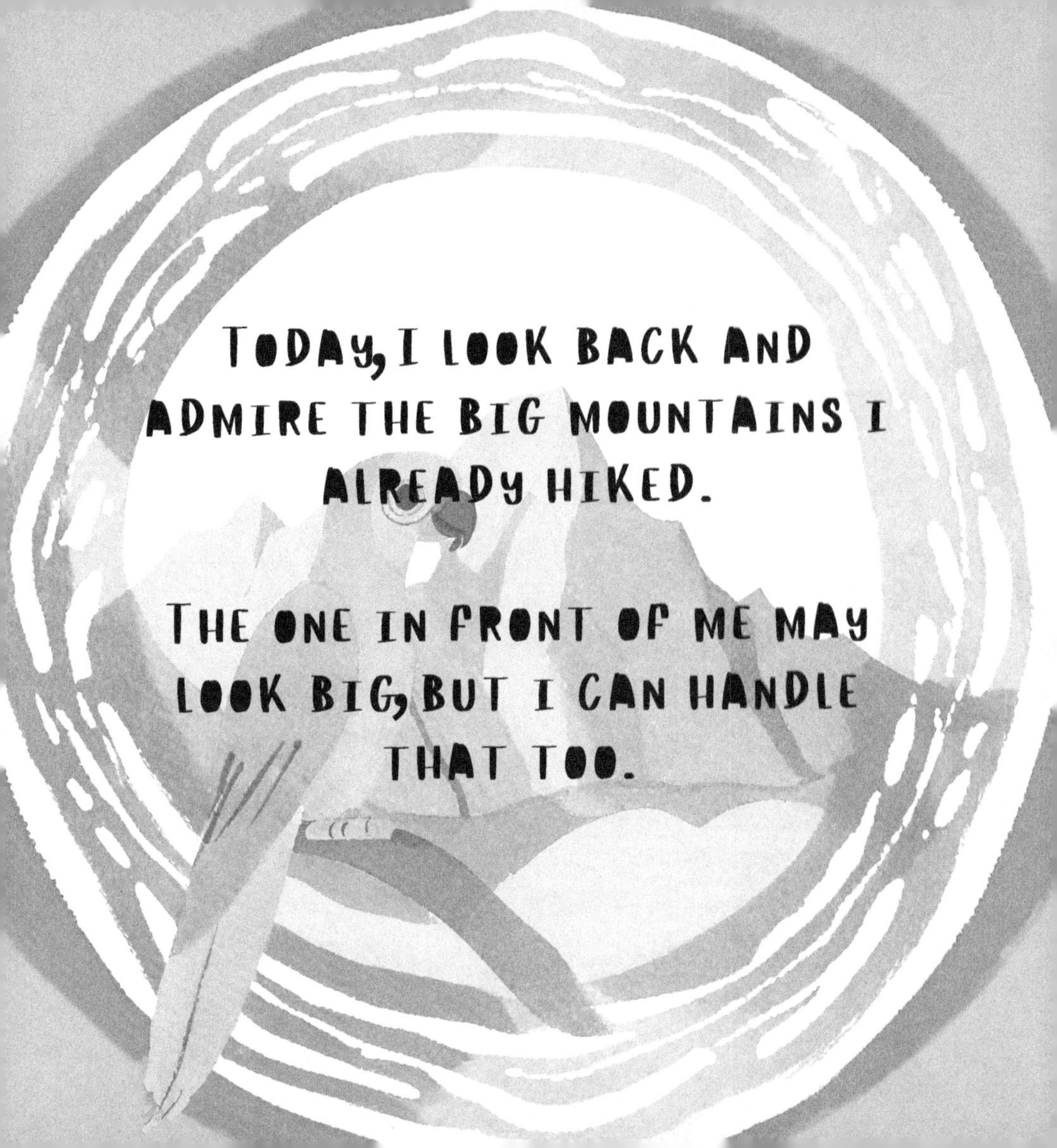

TODAY, I LOOK BACK AND ADMIRE THE BIG MOUNTAINS I ALREADY HIKED.

THE ONE IN FRONT OF ME MAY LOOK BIG, BUT I CAN HANDLE THAT TOO.

THE MOMENT I BELIEVE
THAT I DESERVE BETTER,
THE UNIVERSE CONSPIRES
TO MAKE IT HAPPEN.

ONCE I KNOW WHAT I WANT,
I LET THE UNIVERSE GUIDE ME.
I DON'T CHASE IT,
I SIMPLY LET IT FIND ME.

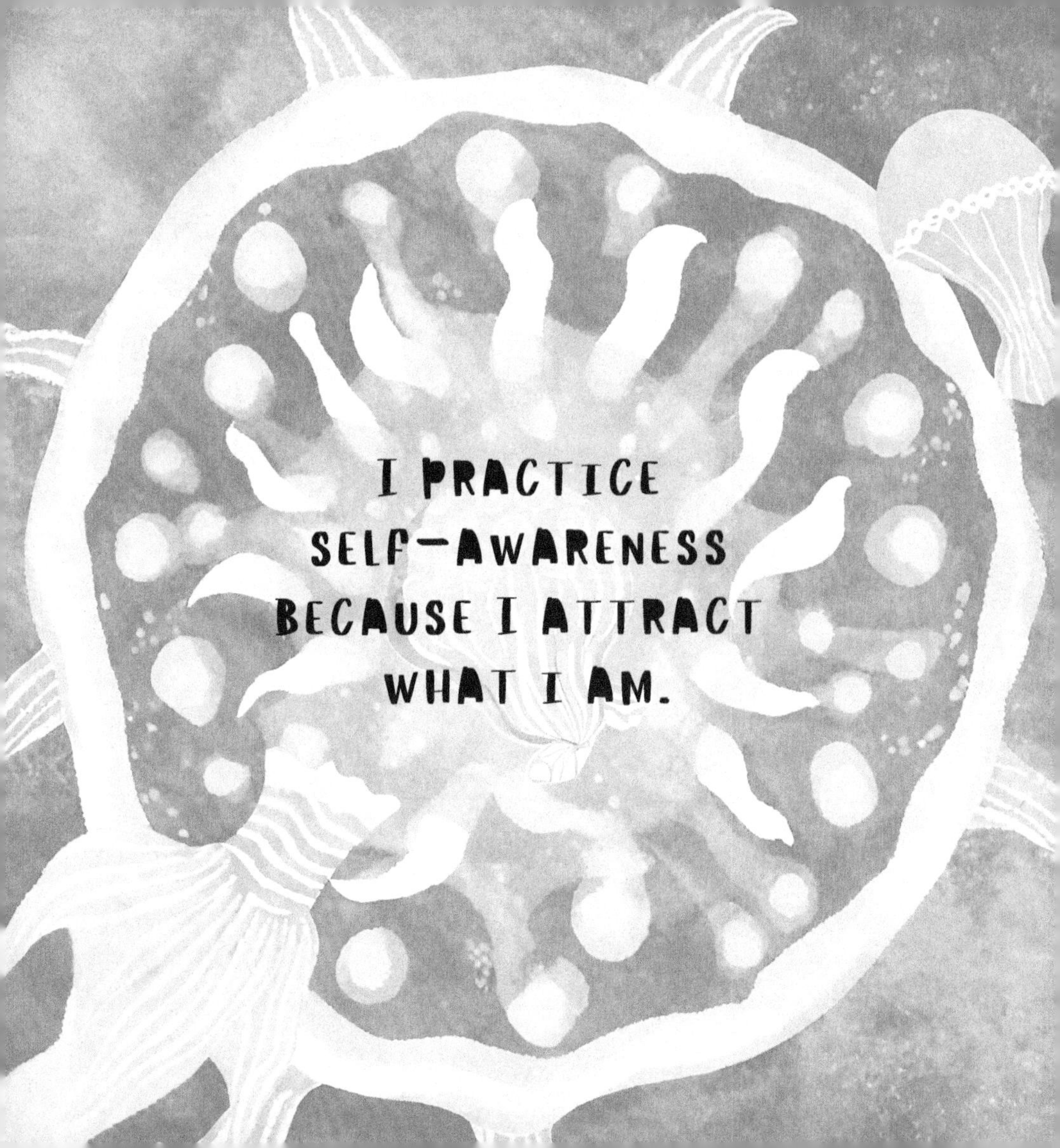
I PRACTICE
SELF-AWARENESS
BECAUSE I ATTRACT
WHAT I AM.

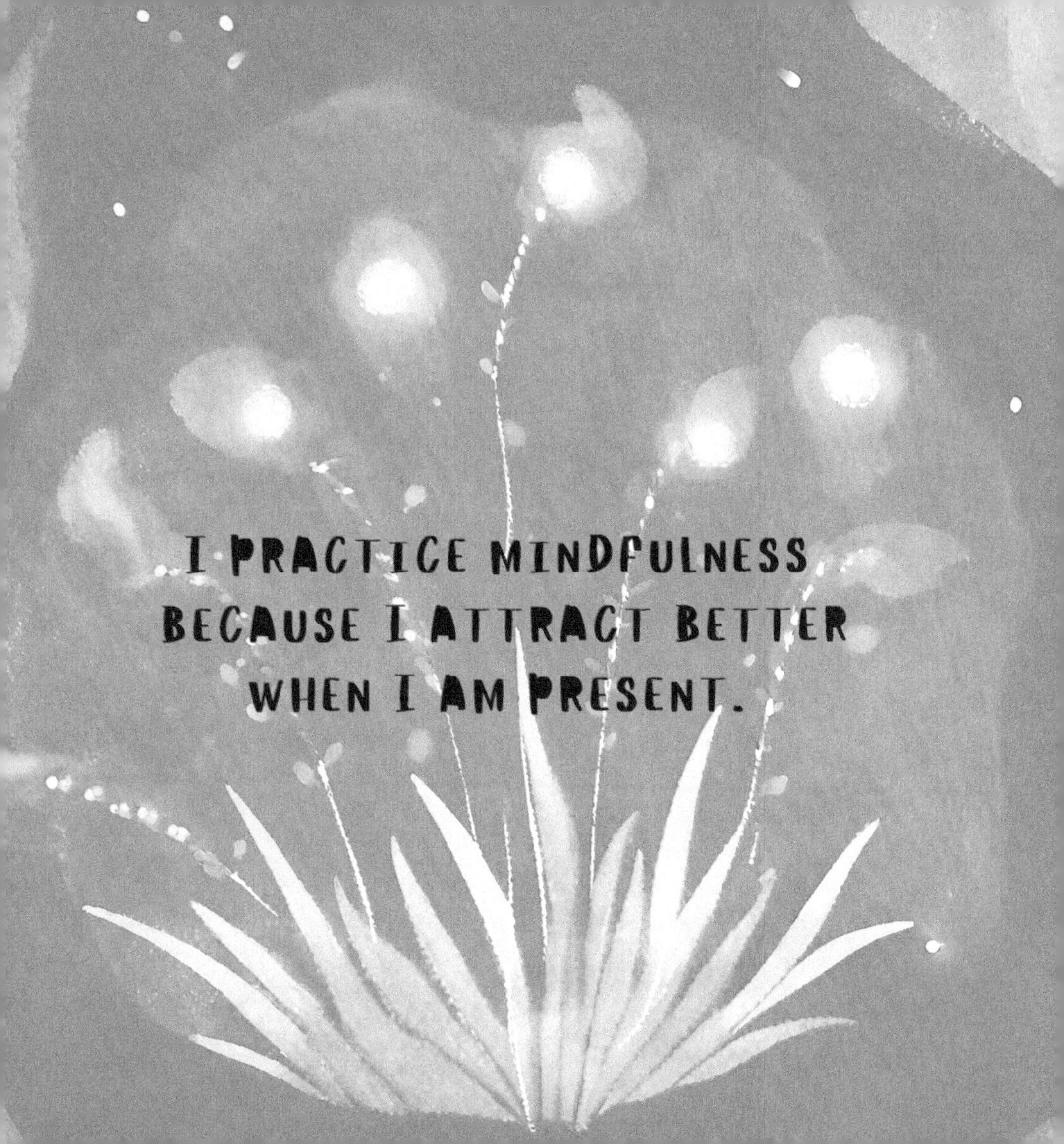
I PRACTICE MINDFULNESS
BECAUSE I ATTRACT BETTER
WHEN I AM PRESENT.

I WILL SEE IT
WHEN I BELIEVE IT.

CULTIVATING A SENSE OF GRATITUDE HELPS ME ACHIEVE MY GOALS FASTER.

WHAT AM I GRATEFUL FOR TODAY?

Being kind
to myself and others
tells my subconscious
that I deserve what I
desire.

I WORK HARDER ON
MYSELF
THAN ON MY PLANS.

EVERY LAYER OF FEAR I SHED
BRINGS ME CLOSER TO
REVEALING MY MOST
POWERFUL VERSION OF MYSELF.
THE TRUE VERSION OF ME.

MY GOALS ARE LIKE TREES.
ONCE THE SEED IS SOWN
THEY TAKE THEIR TIME TO
GROW.

I'M INDIFFERENT
TO THE BURN BENEATH MY FEET
FOR I AM AWARE THAT
I'M SPRINTING
TOWARDS THE SEA.

I'M ALWAYS
BEING GUIDED
TOWARDS MY GOALS.

I UNDERSTAND BETTER
WHEN I'M AT PEACE.

MY INNER WISDOM
IS MUCH MORE POWERFUL
THAN I COULD EVER
IMAGINE.

NOT BECAUSE IT DIDN'T
HAPPEN WHEN I THOUGHT IT
WOULD,
MEANS THAT IT WON'T HAPPEN
AT ALL.

MANIFESTATION IS ONE OF THE SIMPLEST AND MOST INNATE ABILITIES I POSSESS. I AM CONSTANTLY MANIFESTING.

I CHOOSE TO SEE
CHALLENGING SITUATIONS
AS OPPORTUNITIES
TO GROW.

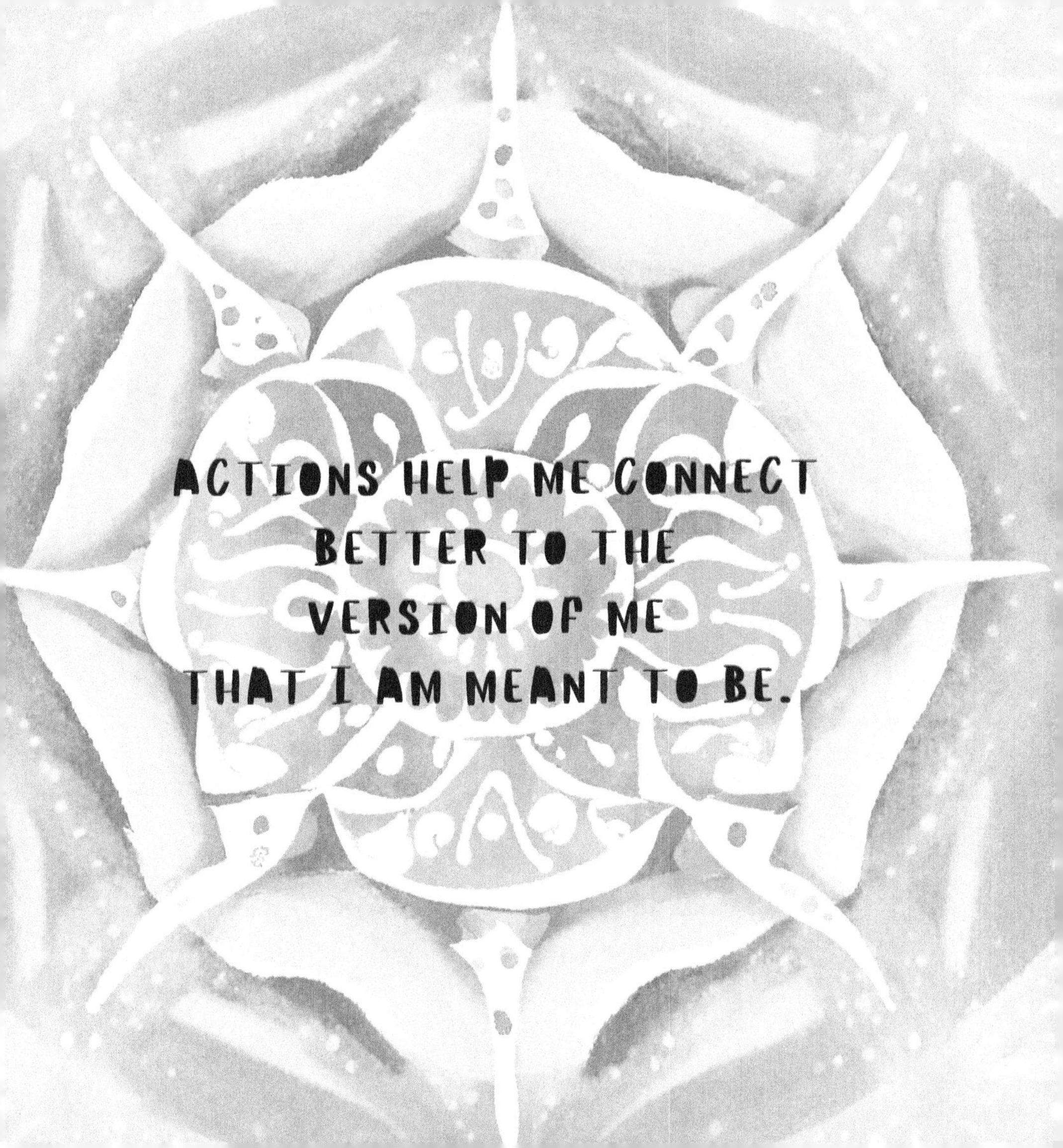
ACTIONS HELP ME CONNECT
BETTER TO THE
VERSION OF ME
THAT I AM MEANT TO BE.

I WILL GET THERE FASTER
WHEN I STOP OVERTHINKING
HOW.

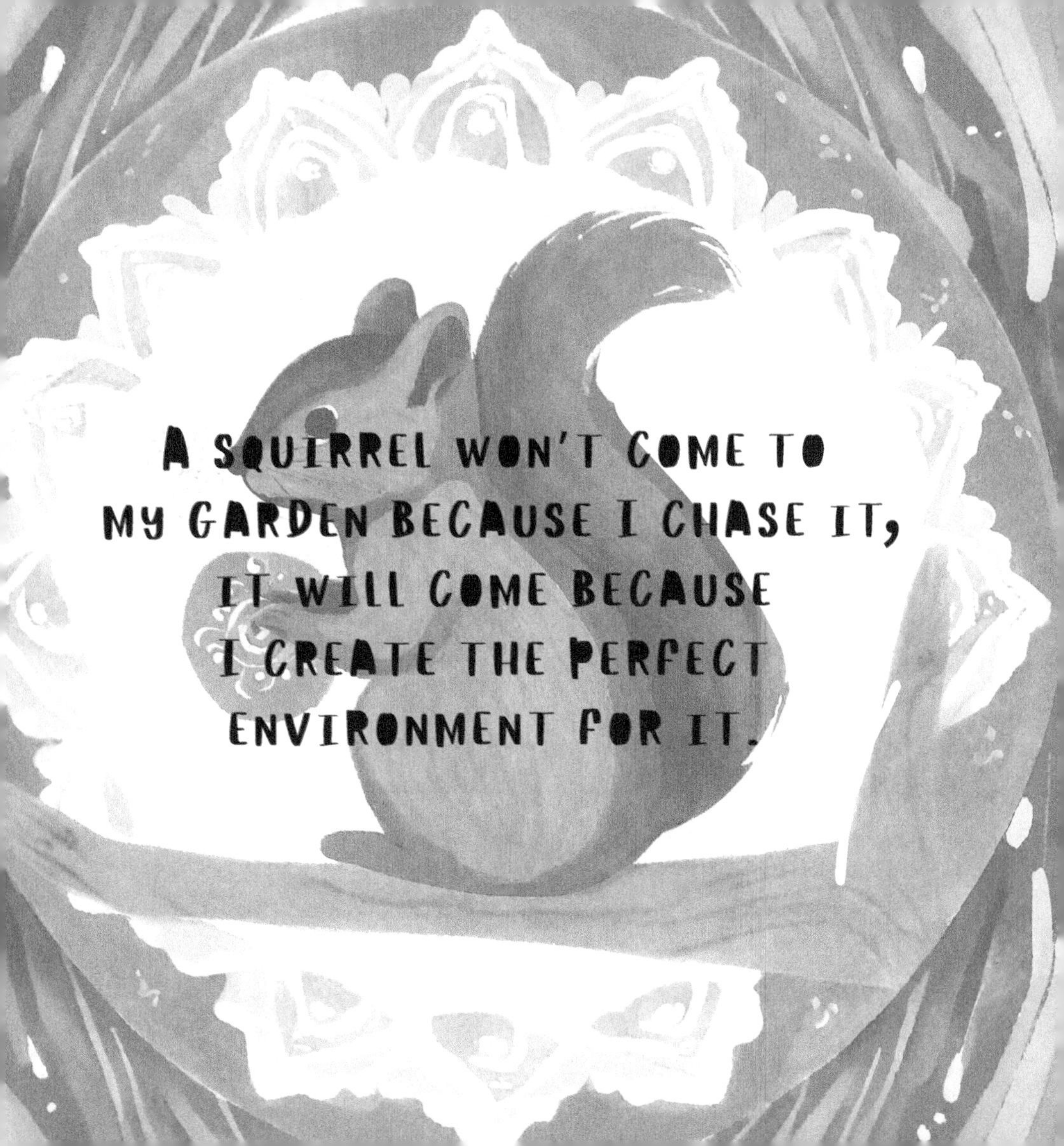

A SQUIRREL WON'T COME TO
MY GARDEN BECAUSE I CHASE IT,
IT WILL COME BECAUSE
I CREATE THE PERFECT
ENVIRONMENT FOR IT.

I BECOME A MAGNET
WHEN I LET
LOVE AND AUTHENTICITY
RUN MY LIFE.

TODAY
I WILL ENGAGE IN
ACTIVITIES
THAT EMPOWER ME.

THE UNIVERSE DOESN'T
HAND ME THE CAKE.
IT PROVIDES
THE INGREDIENTS
TO BAKE IT.

EVERYTHING FALLS INTO PLACE WHEN I LEARN TO MASTER PEACE.

Today,
I won't chase my dreams.
I'll be present and at peace
so that I can tune in
with the guidance
towards them.

TODAY,
I LET GO OF ALL MY FEARS
AND TUNE INTO
MY INNER POWER.

I DECIDE
THE COURSE OF MY LIFE.
THE UNIVERSE
TAKES CARE OF THE REST.

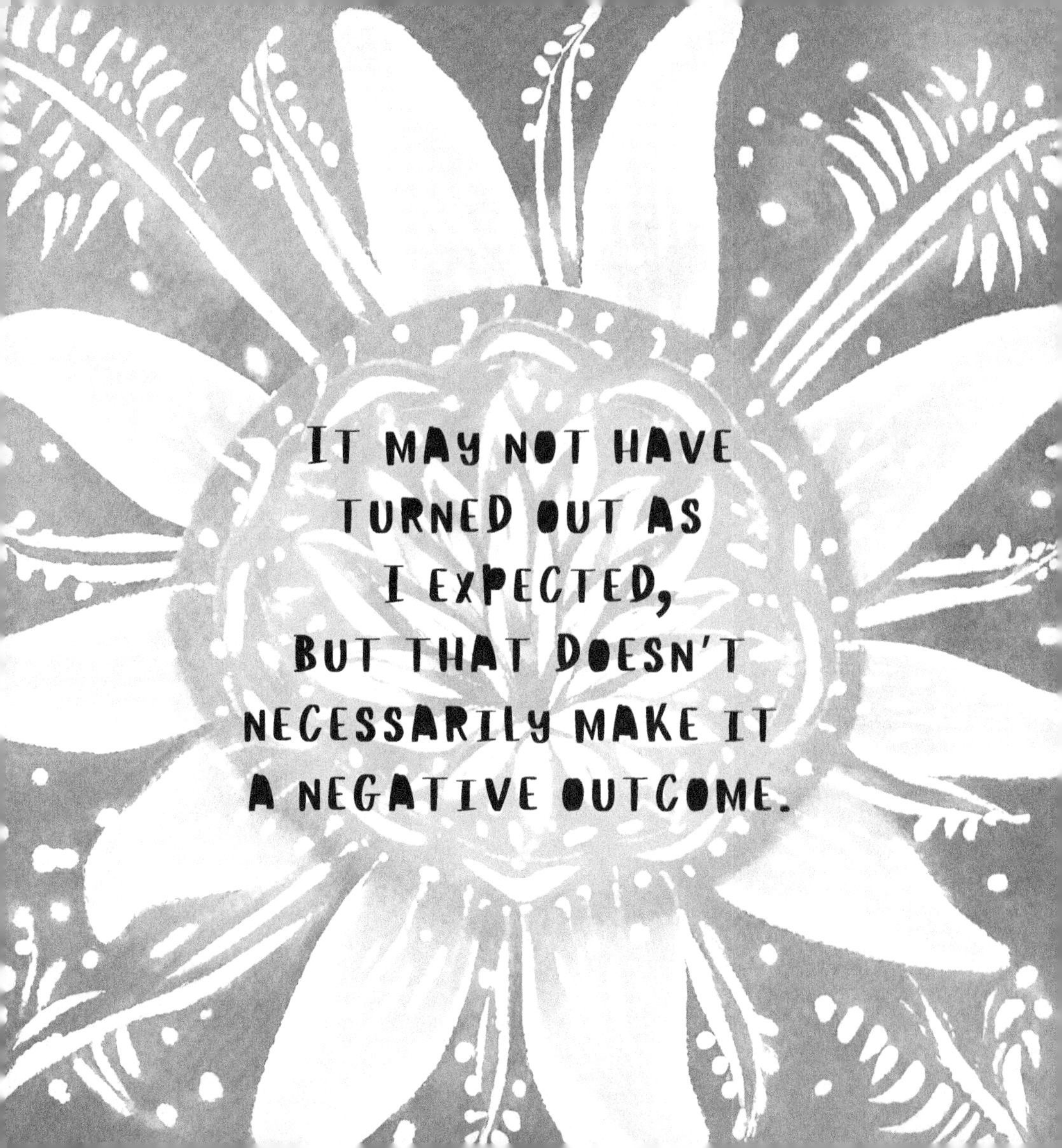

IT MAY NOT HAVE
TURNED OUT AS
I EXPECTED,
BUT THAT DOESN'T
NECESSARILY MAKE IT
A NEGATIVE OUTCOME.

I CHOOSE TO BE HAPPY
NOW.
I RELEASE ALL MY CONCERNS
AND LET MYSELF
BE PRESENT AND AT PEACE.

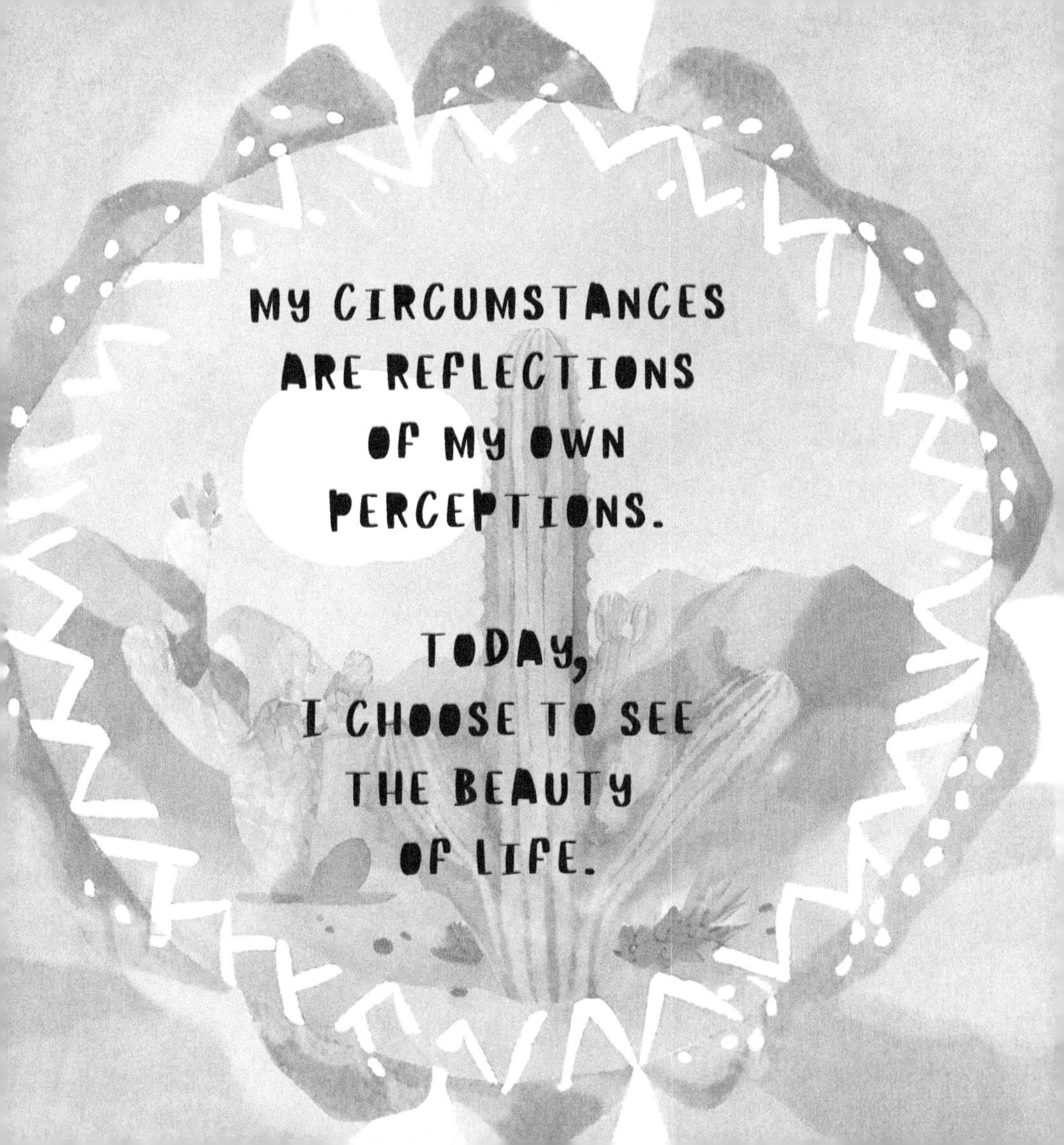

MY CIRCUMSTANCES
ARE REFLECTIONS
OF MY OWN
PERCEPTIONS.

TODAY,
I CHOOSE TO SEE
THE BEAUTY
OF LIFE.

My SUCCESSES
BOOST MY
SELF-CONFIDENCE.
MY CHALLENGES
OFFER
NEW OPPORTUNITIES
TO GROW.

I ENJOY
THE RIDE
AS MUCH AS
THE DESTINATION.

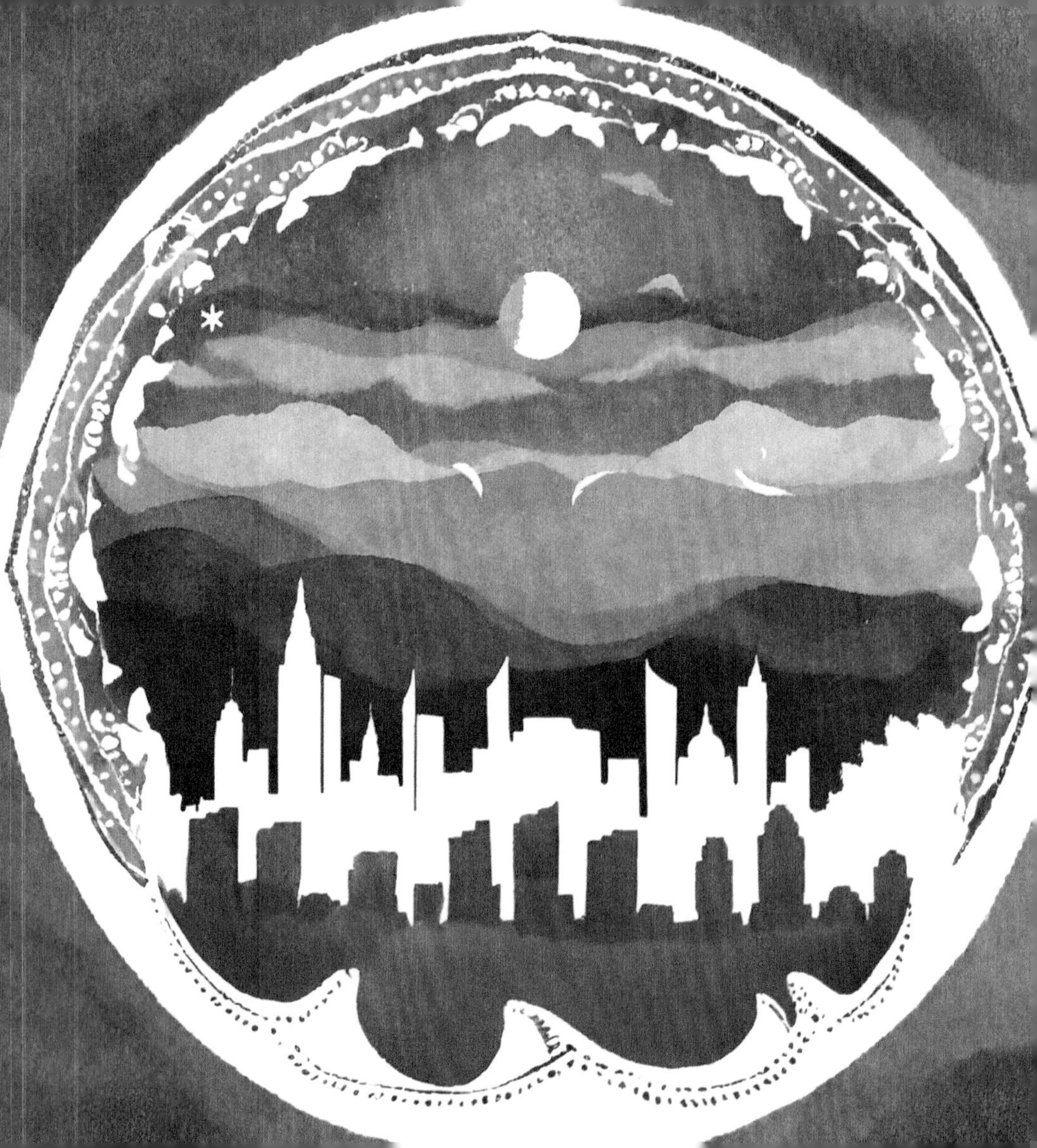

POSITIVE EMOTIONS
ARE THE SWITCH
I CAN USE
TO BECOME MAGNETIC.

MY FREQUENCY
SERVES AS
A COMPASS
TOWARDS MY GOALS.

I BECOME
SUPER MAGNETIC
WHEN I LET
MY FAITH IN THE UNIVERSE
RULE MY LIFE.

MY FREEDOM BEGINS
THE MOMENT I REALIZE
I HAVE THE POWER
TO CHOOSE MY DESTINATION
AND DECIDE
HOW ENJOYABLE
THE JOURNEY IS.

My capacity to see
beauty in things
brings me closer
to my goals.

I AM ALREADY ABUNDANT.

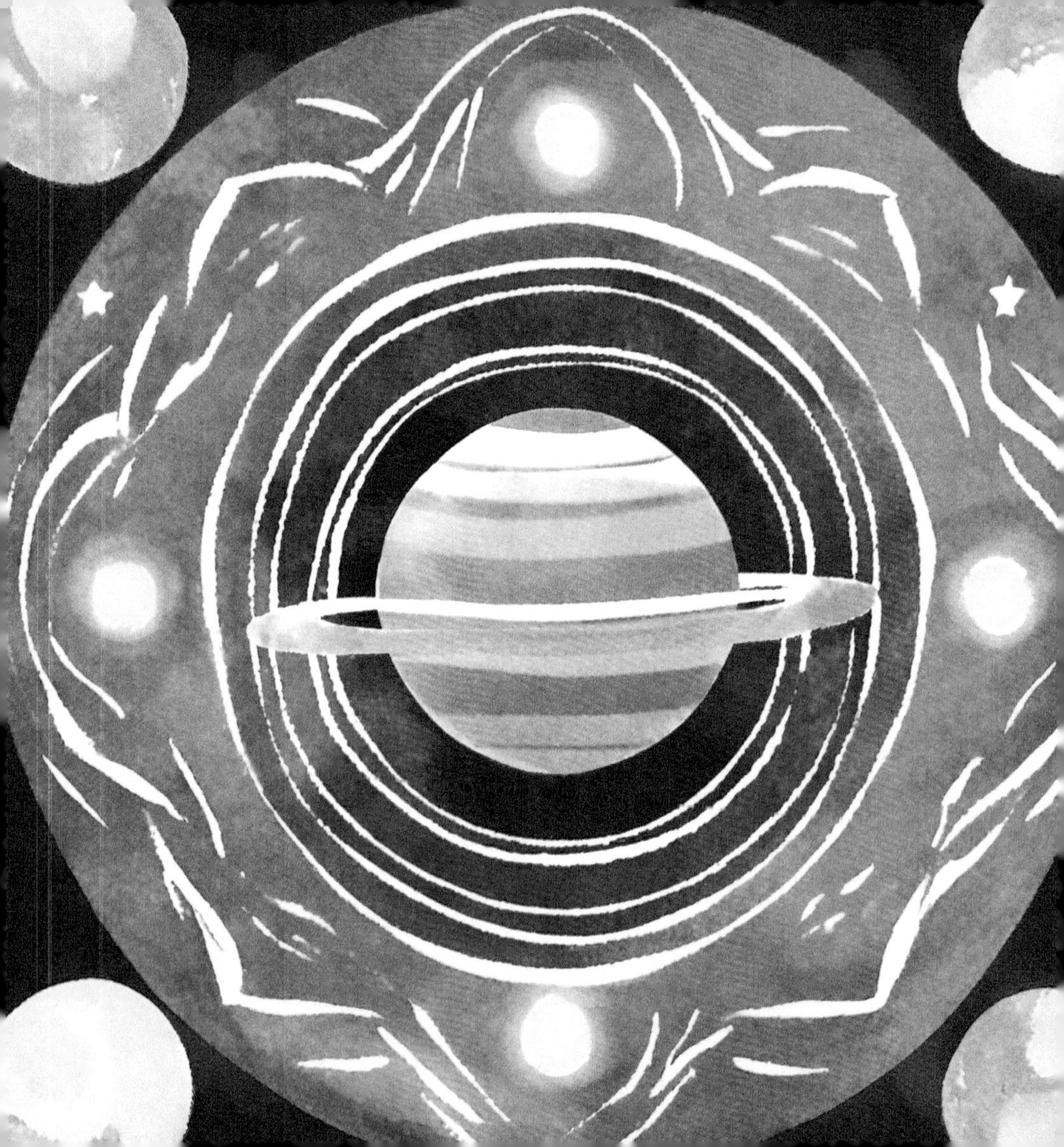

TODAY,
I SURRENDER
I RELEASE MY NEED TO CONTROL
AND LET THE UNIVERSE
DO ITS MAGIC.

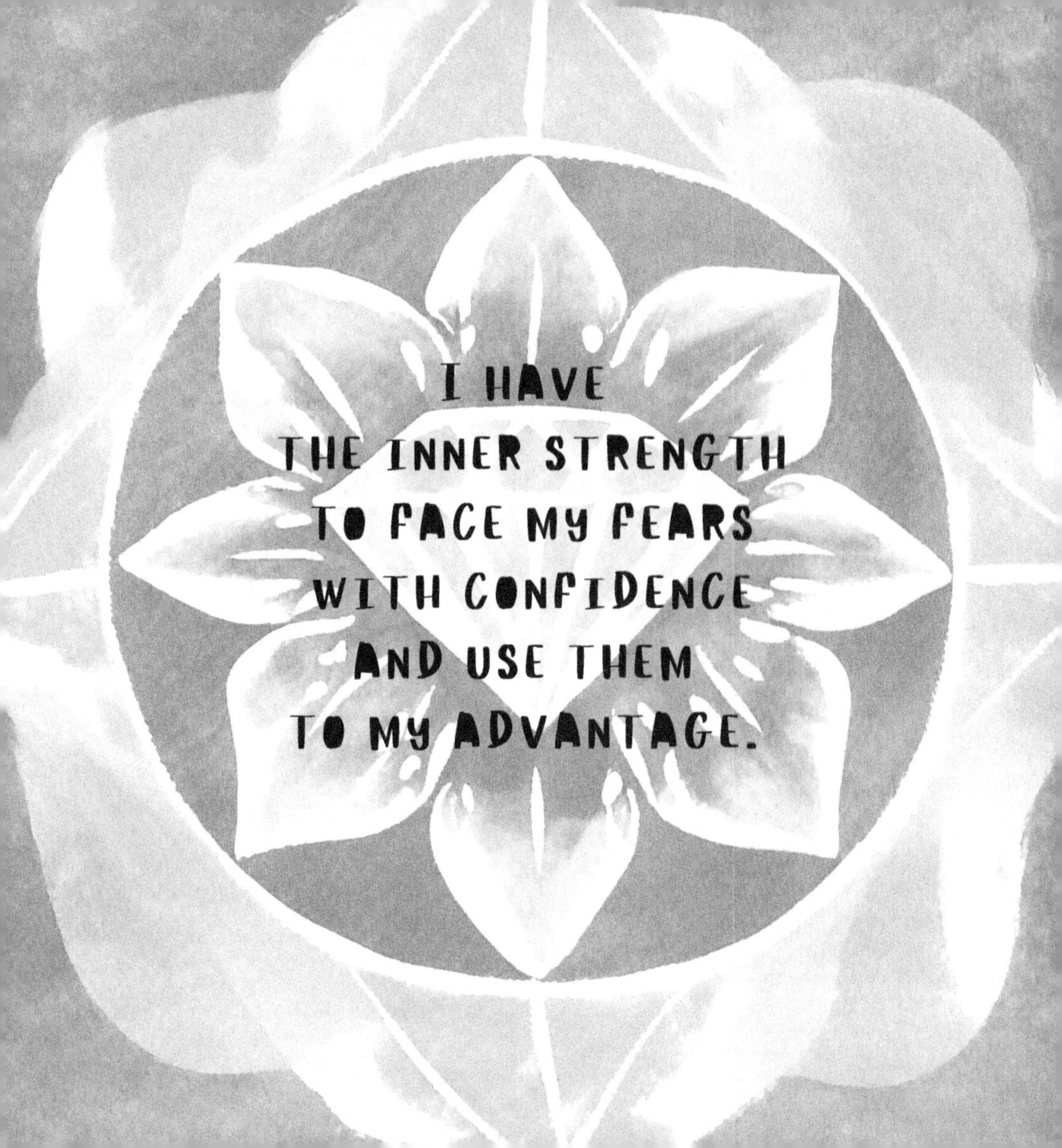
I HAVE
THE INNER STRENGTH
TO FACE MY FEARS
WITH CONFIDENCE
AND USE THEM
TO MY ADVANTAGE.

EVERY PERSON AND
SITUATION IN MY LIFE
IS CONNECTED TO ME
THROUGH MY FREQUENCY.

I TOO WILL HAVE MY
MOMENT TO SHINE.
EVERYTHING HAPPENS
AT THE RIGHT TIME.

MY INNER VOICE ALWAYS GUIDES ME TOWARDS THE RIGHT PATH.
THE MORE I SURRENDER THE LOUDER IT GETS.

WE ALL POSSESS AN INNATE GIFT THAT BENEFITS OURSELVES AND OTHERS.

TODAY,

I CHOOSE TO LOOK DEEP INSIDE MY VERY BEING TO FIND MINE.

I LEARN FROM MY LOSSES
AND UNDERSTAND THAT
THEY ARE OPPORTUNITIES
TO APPRECIATE
AND SURRENDER.

Today,
I'll focus on
expanding my
consciousness
and
awareness.

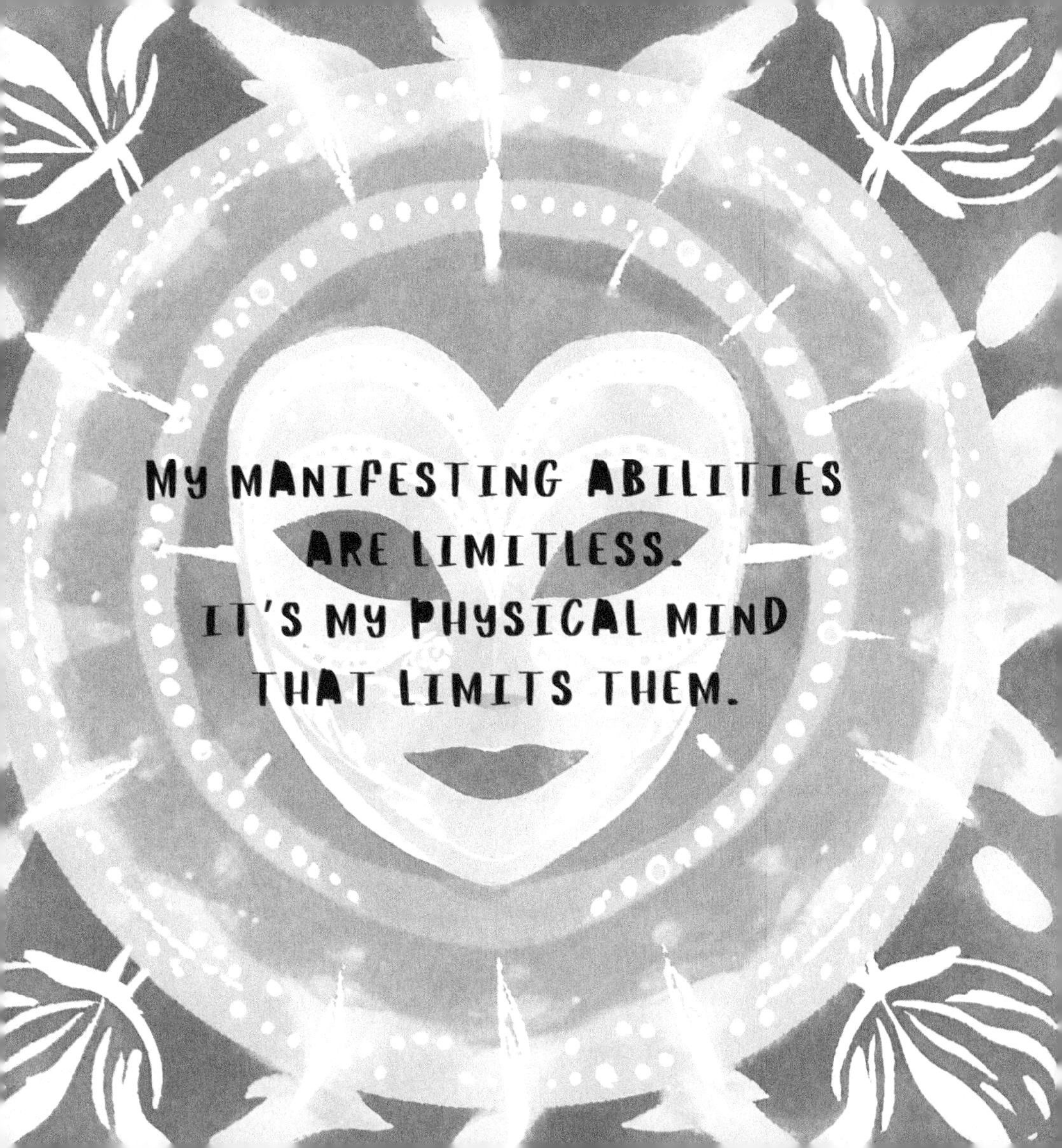
MY MANIFESTING ABILITIES
ARE LIMITLESS.
IT'S MY PHYSICAL MIND
THAT LIMITS THEM.

I ONLY WELCOME
BELIEFS THAT
HELP ME GROW.

I AM OPEN TO
THE SIGNS THE
UNIVERSE
PROVIDES DAILY.

I USE TOOLS LIKE MUSIC TO RAISE MY VIBRATION AND FREQUENCY.

THE MORE I RUSH
THE LESS I CAN SEE.

I DON'T WALK TOWARDS
MY GOALS.
THEY COME TO ME.

I only work on it
after I feel
grounded and at peace.

TODAY,
I NURTURE MY INNER CHILD
AND REGULATE MY ENERGY
TO ATTRACT BETTER

I LOOK DEEP
INSIDE MY VERY BEING
TO CHECK ON MY FREQUENCY
AND ADJUST IT ACCORDINGLY.

I USE LAUGHTER
TO RAISE MY
VIBRATION
AND ATTRACT
BETTER.

I AM MEANT TO
HAVE FUN.
LIFE ISN'T SUPPOSED
TO BE SO SERIOUS.

I REMEMBER TO STOP
AND ADMIRE THE BEAUTY
AROUND ME.

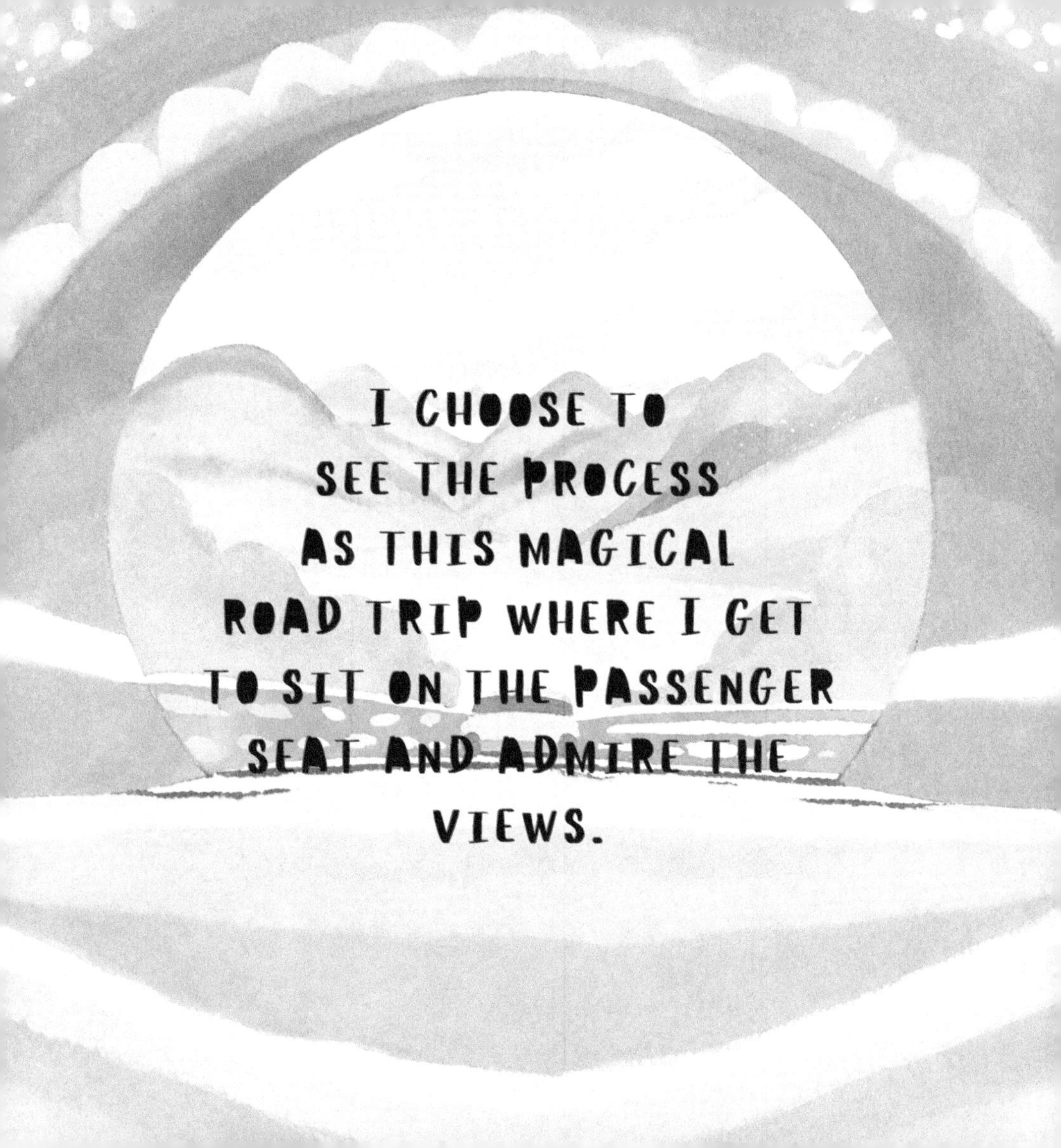

I CHOOSE TO
SEE THE PROCESS
AS THIS MAGICAL
ROAD TRIP WHERE I GET
TO SIT ON THE PASSENGER
SEAT AND ADMIRE THE
VIEWS.

MY WORST
MOMENTS SHAPE ME.
I CHOOSE TO LET
THEM SHAPE ME
IN A POSITIVE
WAY.

I NURTURE MYSELF
EVERY MORNING,
SO THAT I CAN START
THE DAY WITH THE
RIGHT FREQUENCY

WHEN I FEEL,
I EXPERIENCE.
I CAN'T WISH
FOR SOMETHING
I'M ALREADY
EXPERIENCING.

Any moment
and any situation
can be used
to stop and meditate.

I OPEN MY DOOR
TO THE RIGHT PEOPLE
AND SITUATIONS.

TODAY,
I WILL DO ONE
THING THAT TAKES
ME OUT OF MY
COMFORT ZONE.

I DON'T CHASE A
SPECIFIC FREQUENCY.
I TUNE TO MY HIGHER SELF
AND MAINTAIN MY ENERGY
SO THAT I CAN ATTRACT
WHAT'S IN ALIGNMENT.

IT'S NOT HAPPENING
TO ME.
IT'S HAPPENING
FOR ME.

TODAY,
I WILL TAKE A MINUTE
TO LIST 5 THINGS
I'M GRATEFUL FOR NOW.

WHEN I AM MYSELF,
I ATTRACT
THE RIGHT PEOPLE
AND SITUATIONS
AND EVERYTHING
FALLS INTO PLACE.

MY INTUITION
IS MY HIGHER SELF'S VOICE.
WHEN I LISTEN TO IT
I ATTRACT WHAT'S
RIGHT FOR ME.

The Universe
will reveal its
secrets to me
once I start
to fully trust life
and tame my fears.

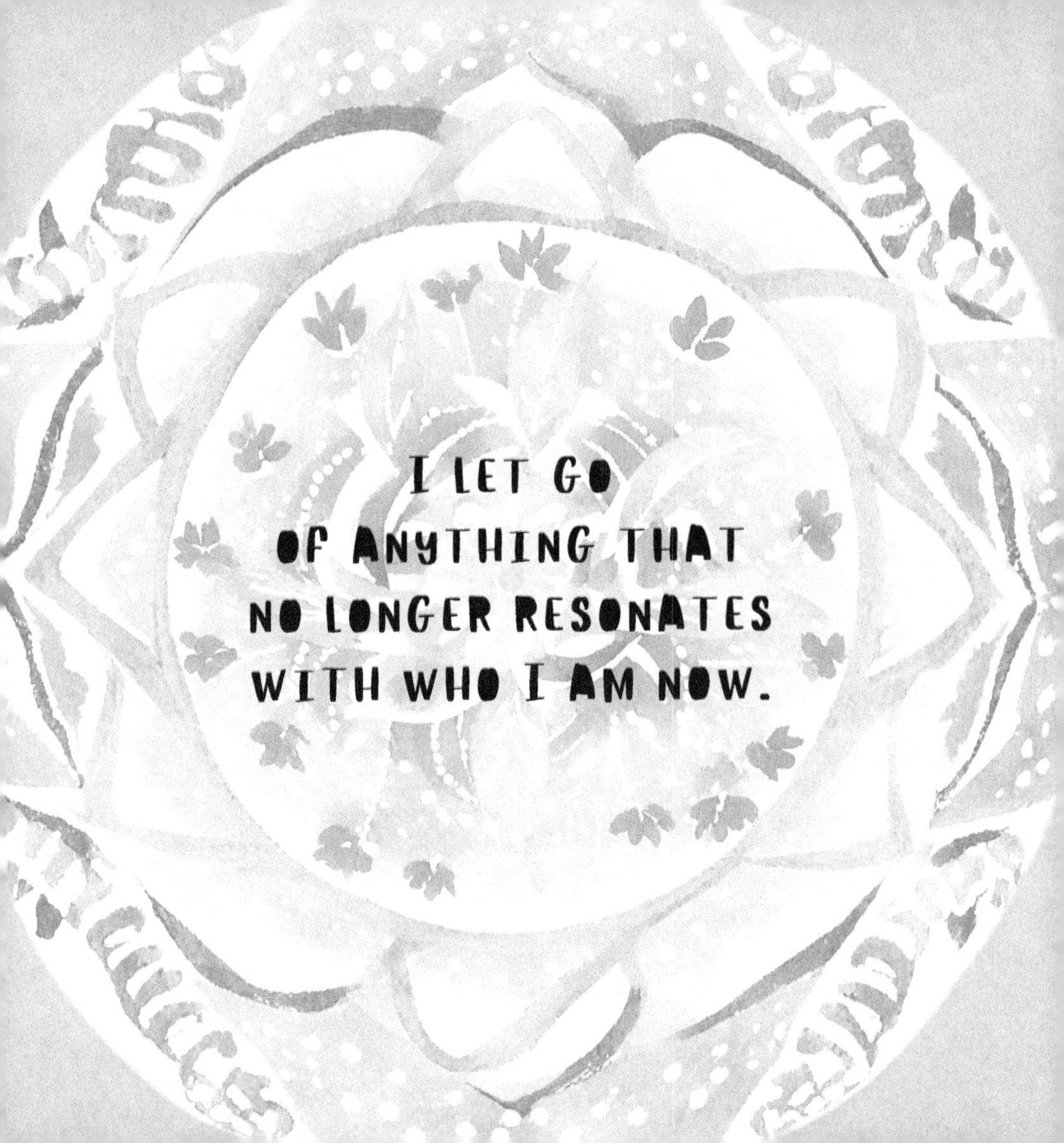
I LET GO
OF ANYTHING THAT
NO LONGER RESONATES
WITH WHO I AM NOW.

LIFE BECOMES
FUN AND EASY
WHEN I LET GO
OF CONTROL.

WHEN I CONTROL
MY EMOTIONAL STATE,
I CONTROL MY
BEHAVIORS,
HENCE MY RESULTS.

Sometimes,
it's better to let
the current
take me.

I TAKE DAY-TO-DAY
ACTIONS
THAT BRING ME
CLOSER TO MY GOALS.

HAVE I
RESTED ENOUGH
TO DO MY MOST
LOVING MEANINGFUL
WORK?

I GROW
WHEN I USE MY
GREATEST POTENTIAL
AND FACE MY
DARKEST SHADOW.

The ultimate
purpose of my goals
is how they will
make me feel.
Therefore,
I manifest the
feelings
and not the goal.

PRACTICING
SELF-LOVE
AND GRATITUDE
ON A DAILY BASIS
BRINGS ME CLOSER
TO MY GOALS.

THE MORE
ATTENTION I PAY
TO SYNCHRONICITIES,
THE MORE
SYNCHRONICITIES
I EXPERIENCE.

I ATTRACT PEOPLE
WHO SERVE
MY HIGHER GOOD.

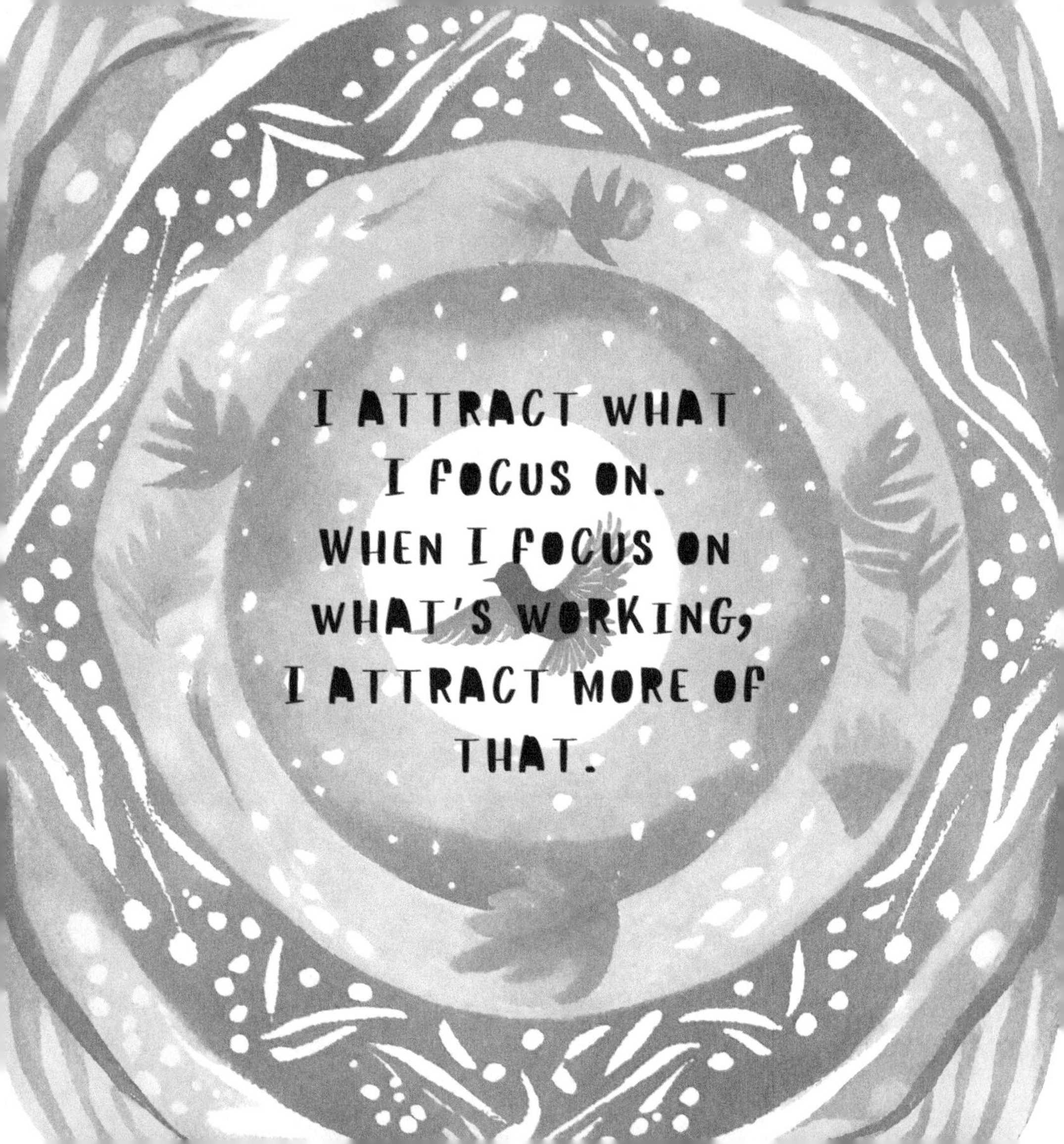
I ATTRACT WHAT
I FOCUS ON.
WHEN I FOCUS ON
WHAT'S WORKING,
I ATTRACT MORE OF
THAT.

Today,
I let go of control
and let
faith and desire
take charge.

SOMETIMES
GOING SLOWER
IS ALL I NEED.

MY FAITH
KEEPS ME GROUNDED.
MY ACTIONS
KEEP ME EXCITED.
MY EXCITEMENT
KEEPS THE FREQUENCY
I DESIRE.

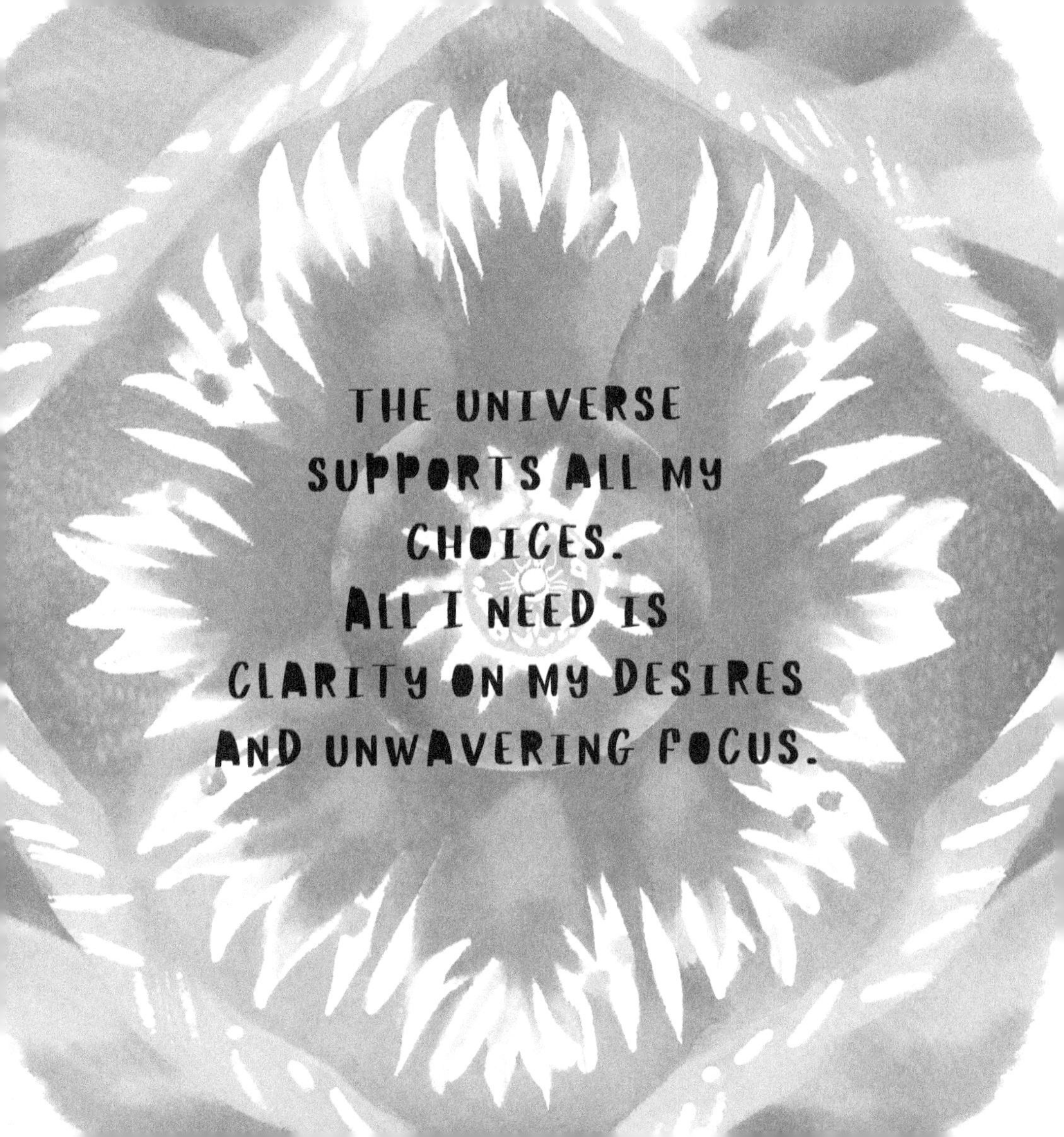
THE UNIVERSE
SUPPORTS ALL MY
CHOICES.
ALL I NEED IS
CLARITY ON MY DESIRES
AND UNWAVERING FOCUS.

I CALIBRATE
MY ENERGY
WITH
LOVE AND JOY.

WHEN I'M STILL,
I LISTEN
AND UNDERSTAND.

WHEN I'M HAPPY
AND AT PEACE,
MY PLANS BECOME
THE UNIVERSE'S PLANS.

I MAKE JOY
MY PRIORITY.

I RELEASE WHAT
DOESN'T BRING ME JOY.